RAPPORT

Rapport | Gabriel Angelo

RAPPORT

The Art of Connecting with People and Building Relationships

GABRIEL ANGELO

SN & NS
PUBLICATIONS

Copyright © SN & NS Publications

All rights reserved.

It is impermissible to reproduce any part of this book without prior consent. All violations will be prosecuted to the fullest extent of the law.

While attempts have been made to verify the information contained within this publication, neither the author nor the publisher assumes any responsibility for errors, omissions, interpretation or usage of the subject matter herein.

This publication contains the opinions and ideas of its author and is intended for informational purpose only. The author and publisher shall in no event be held liable for any loss or other damages incurred from the usage of this publication.

ISBN 978-1-535-09777-2

Printed in the United States of America

First Edition

CONTENTS

Introduction
- 9 -

Chapter 1
The Importance of Rapport
- 11 -

Chapter 2
The Science of Rapport
- 15 -

Chapter 3
The Development of Rapport
- 21 -

Chapter 4
The Relationships of Rapport
- 42 -

Chapter 5
The Applications of Rapport

- 52 -

Chapter 6
The Practices of Rapport

- 65 -

Chapter 7
The Establishment of Rapport

- 71 -

Rapport | Gabriel Angelo

Rapport | Gabriel Angelo

Introduction

Have you ever had the experience of just meeting someone, and two minutes later being as comfortable with them as if you've known them forever, like your best friend? Or how about the famed "Romeo and Juliet" meeting, when they met for a moment and just *knew*? This can happen as blinding as it did to each of them, or so subtly that only later do you realize how well you connect.

This event, in various forms, strengths, and permutations, occurs all over the world, every second of the day. Great romances, passionate friendships, and deep bonds of brotherhood can be formed out of the first, lightning-quick response to another person. There are people who have this experience constantly, and they can seem to live a charmed life, effortlessly creating deep, lasting connections and reaping the benefits those connections provide.

What if someone told you that you could be one of these people? That the magic charm is something that can be practiced and learned? Whoever it is, this person would tell you that these great friendships, romances, bonds, and the charmed life of those who have them is due to a single concept - **rapport**.

Chapter 1
The Importance of Rapport

What is a rapport? Rapport is a positive connection with another person, one that involves caring and understanding. The Merriam-Webster dictionary defines rapport as "relation characterized by harmony, conformity, accord, or affinity."

Rapport can happen immediately when you meet someone - the famous "clicking" - or develop slowly through multiple interactions and conversations with another person. Rapport occurs between two people. You cannot develop rapport on your own. It requires both parties to be willing to connect and make the effort or take the actions necessary to make that connection happen.

Rapport is by definition a positive connection. An intense, immediate connection that is negative - a "reverse clicking" - is not a rapport. A rapport is created by a positive reaction towards the other person on both sides, and a mutual interest, caring, and understanding. This interest, caring, and understanding is the basis on which a deeper relationship can be built. It is a surface-level connection, that has the potential for further connection. Rapport is created by the understanding on both sides that the other person finds them interesting, that they have things in common, that they understand the other (as far as such a surface connection goes) and that each person cares for the well-being of the other.

Furthermore, rapport occurs when people's communication styles match and they are on the same wavelength. People who are naturally good at establishing rapport can easily recognize and adapt to the other person's style of communication. This means, for example, that someone who is highly energetic and talks and thinks in short, high-energy bursts will probably not develop rapport with someone whose communication style is more verbose and wandering, and has a tendency to lecture. For these people to establish rapport, they need to be able to adapt to the way the other communicates, so that they are speaking in the same language style as each other.

To become expert at building rapport, you have to practice making the other person the center of attention and adapting to make sure that they are as comfortable as possible within a given situation.

We All Want to Connect

All humans crave to connect. We need relationships with other people, whether they are with family, friends, significant others, or coworkers. Rapport is one of the most fundamental building blocks of relationships. However, rapport is not only the foundation of successful relationships, it is also the foundation of broader success. Rapport at work, with clients, bosses, and coworkers, make it more likely for you to cooperate and get assist on large projects, do the best work that you can, and get and keep clients if you are in a client- or customer-facing position.

Not only will rapport help you succeed in your job, it will help you get your job in the first place. Professionals on both sides of the desk in a hiring interview emphasize the importance of building a rapport; from the interviewer's side, rapport is important to relax the interviewee and get a more accurate impression of their personality and skills, and from the job applicant's side, it is important to help him or her impress and stand out to the interviewer so they are more likely to hire the applicant.

There is a common mental image of someone walking to an interview, saying that they went to the same school as the interviewer, and getting a slap on the back and a "You're hired!" What this is, is an instant rapport based on a very strong common bond - the experience of attending that particular school. While you cannot guarantee that you went to the same school as a hiring manager or that such school-based rapport will be so powerful, you can develop your ability to generate rapport to be a valuable asset in job hunting and working life.

Chapter 2
The Science of Rapport

It's common knowledge that when two people encounter each other, they can instantly "click." This immediate bonding with another person is the result of an instant rapport, a connection between the individuals.

Rapport is the foundation of relationships and communication, and so it is in people's best interest to develop rapport whenever possible. There are some people who develop rapport with others wherever they go, and these people tend to be extremely successful. To duplicate this success, scientists, psychologists, businesspeople and others have investigated the secrets and science behind building rapport, and found some common themes that allow rapport to be created and duplicated by anyone who studies and applies their findings.

What Creates Rapport?

Linda Tickle-Degnen and Robert Rosenthal from Boston University and Harvard University explored the subject of rapport and published their findings in their article "The Nature of Rapport and Its Nonverbal Correlates." They found that rapport isn't something that one person intrinsically has, it's something that only happens when two people interact. This means that rapport isn't some kind of inborn talent, like perfect pitch, but something that be created. Some people may have a talent for it from the start, but it's something that can be developed and nurtured like any other talent.

In their research, Tickle-Degnen and Rosenthal identified three basic components of rapport: mutual attentiveness, positivity, and coordination.

For rapport to exist, both people interacting need to be focused on each other, and be interested in what the other is saying or doing. This attention also needs to be positive. Two people can be very focused on each other with the intent of tearing each other down, but this will not create rapport. Each individual needs to approach the interaction positively, with friendliness and caring about what the other has to say.

Finally, a large part of rapport depends on coordination. Coordination means that the biological aspects of the interaction need to be balanced. To build rapport, people need to match each other's energy level, body language, tone, and talking speed. Imagine a conversation between two interested positive people, but one person is turned away from the other, and one is talking very quickly and the other is talking slowly. They are unlikely to build a rapport, because their body language, energy level, and talking speed are out of sync.

More recent studies have suggested that the coordination aspect of rapport is even more important in the early stages of rapport-building than previously supposed, and the importance decreases when the rapport is more firmly established. Indicators include the study "Strangers in sync: Achieving embodied rapport through shared movements" by Tanya Vacharkulksemsuk, M.A. and Barbara L. Fredrickson, Ph.D.

This makes sense; when you have established a strong bond, it is less important to make sure that your physical expression and movements reflect those of the person with whom you are interacting.

For instance, if you are just meeting someone, your facial expressions and physicality need to mirror theirs to establish a rapport. However, if you are interacting with a friend, someone with whom you already have a strong rapport and a developed bond, your relationship with them will depend less on your body language. The physical aspect of rapport is extremely important in the first establishment of rapport, and the importance decreases as the relationship develops, though this does not mean that your body language and expression can be dismissive, inattentive, or negative. These negative behaviors will diminish or threaten your rapport no matter how strong the existing bond may be.

The Study of Rapport

With the importance of rapport, it's no wonder that it's been the focus of a great deal of scrutiny and study. However, this respect for rapport as a subject worthy of study has been comparatively recent.

In their article "Rapport is Not So Soft Anymore" Bella DePaulo and Kathy Bell from the University of Virginia noted that "For a long time, rapport was just so mushy that serious scientists were a little embarrassed to be associated with it professionally, much as they may have enjoyed a bit of indulgence in private"

(Psychological Inquiry: An International Journal for the Advancement of Psychological Theory Volume 1, Issue 4, 1990 p.305).

However, this started to change when Linda Tickle-Degnen and Robert Rosenthal published their work exploring and defining the nature of rapport. Their approach to rapport as a legitimate subject of study helped to open the playing field for researchers in more fields to investigate rapport itself and its effects. Studies on the effect of rapport between patients and doctors were actually published long before the Tickle-Degnen and Rosenthal studies were published.

As early as the 1960s, researchers reported that surgical patients who had a strong rapport with their doctors experienced reduced pain after operations, such as in the 1964 study "Reduction of Postoperative Pain by Encouragement and Instruction of Patients - A Study of Doctor-Patient Rapport" by Lawrence D. Egbert, M.D., George E. Battit, M.D., Claude E. Welch, M.D., and Marshall K. Bartlett, M.D., which was published in the New England Journal of Medicine. Studies on doctor-patient rapport, teacher-student rapport, and therapist/psychologist-patient rapport were the most common, and each cited the importance of rapport for the effectiveness of the relationship, the effectiveness of the treatment, and the effectiveness of teaching.

Over the past several decades, the study of rapport has continued to develop as a recognized and legitimate subject of study. Researchers and practitioners in more areas studied, researched and published on the effect of rapport. Today, there are tens of thousands of articles and studies worldwide on the effects of rapport in such different fields as medicine, law, diplomacy, and hostage negotiation, to name only a few.

Rapport itself, its cause, and its nature are also fair game for investigation. Studies such as "The Biological Basis of Rapport" by Michael Argyle, "The Nature of Rapport" by Clyde Hendrick, and "Measuring Rapport" by Starkey Duncan Jr. all approach rapport as a measurable, repeatable, and learnable part of human interaction.

Chapter 3
The Development of Rapport

Rapport can be built naturally and without intent, but it is best to go about building rapport deliberately and thoughtfully, so that you can duplicate the rapport effect with as many people as you want to. You build rapport verbally and non-verbally, and the non-verbal aspect is just as important as the verbal component.

We'll break down the two components below.

Non-verbal

Non-verbal rapport building consists of matching non-verbal signals and body language, like position and movement, eye contact, and facial expression.

To really build a rapport, you need to match what the other person's body is telling you, and make sure that your body is telling them that you are interested in them and invested in the interaction. Keeping your body open and relaxed, smiling, and keeping your head and body turned towards the person you're interacting with all assist in projecting interest and attentiveness.

Your tone of voice and speech pace are also essential elements in non-verbal rapport building. Talking quickly at a high pitch can convey stress, which makes it more difficult to develop a rapport because the other person picks up on your stress and will most likely become stressed themselves. Moderating your tone and keeping your speech relatively slow, but still invested with energy is the best way to use your voice (without words) to build a rapport with someone.

A non-verbal aspect of rapport-building that is less often discussed than tone and body language, but is equally important, is energy level. To establish a rapport with someone, you need to match the energy, enthusiasm, and feeling of "aliveness" that they put out.

Imagine watching two people interact. They are facing each other and mirroring their body language, talking and smiling, but one gives off an incredible energy and enthusiasm, and one is lethargic and dull. They are not matching their energy level, and they are unlikely to build as strong a rapport as two people who were matching energy level would.

Energy level can be a conscious decision; you can decide to be energetic and enthusiastic when you talking to someone, even if you were not feeling that way initially. It is no different than deciding to match their speech patterns, or maintaining eye contact.

Verbal

The verbal component of rapport is the conversation, what you say to another person to develop a rapport. To build a rapport, you need to establish common ground with the other person, and make them feel that you are genuinely interested in them and what they have to say.

The best way to convey interest in a person is to let them speak. Ask the other person questions, and genuinely listen to their answers, then let the other person know that you heard them, usually by restating what they said or by asking another question that follows up on what they said. Restating what they said also allows you to use their language back at them, creating a continual impression of common ground.

Shared experiences and opinions are often the basis of quick rapport, such as when two people find out they attended the same college, were in the same club, or are rabid fans of the same sports team. That commonality creates an instant bond, and to achieve that you want to find ways that you are the person talking to you are alike or share interests.

An important part of verbal rapport is empathy. Empathy is putting yourself in someone else's shoes to get a sense of their experience or feelings. Empathy is not 'feeling for' it is 'feeling with.' Putting yourself in someone's shoes during a conversation conveys that you genuinely care for them, and people respond well to that caring. It is important, however, that the interest and caring that you convey be at least partly genuine.

Building a rapport is one of the building blocks of a relationship, and particularly is this relationship is intended to be long term or ongoing, building the relationship on false pretenses is not a good idea.

Proven Rapport Building Techniques

Since rapport is something you can learn, there are a number of proven techniques you can use to maximize your rapport with another person during an interaction. These techniques include:

- **Mirroring**

Mirroring is both verbal and physical. To use verbal mirroring, which is also called 'reframing,' you take what the person you are talking to says, summarize it, and say it back to them.

If they told you about their experience mountain climbing in Peru, for example, you could reflect it and say "So, you went to Peru for two weeks and the mountain-climbing was amazing," then go on to ask follow up questions.

This verbal mirroring performs two tasks; it ensures that you got the gist of the story correct by giving you a chance to confirm your impression and for them to correct you, and it confirms to them that you have been listening and paying attention to what they've been saying.

Physical mirroring goes back to our previous discussion of body language and rapport. While you don't want to mimic what the other person is doing exactly, you want to sync up your body language to theirs, from movement to tone to facial expression. Reflecting both their own body language and verbal language back to them puts you both on the same wavelength, and helps to foster a rapport.

Corporate Support Services, LLC has a great list things to keep in mind when mirroring. These include:

- **Facial Expressions** - smiling, frowning, looking concerned or excited, etc.
- **Gestures** - gesturing or waving your arms or hands and you speak
- **Eye movements** - widening or narrowing your eyes or looking elsewhere as you or the other person speaks to emphasize a point or indicate an emotional response.
- **Head movement and tilt** - tilting your head towards someone is an indication of trust.
- **How close you are to the other person** – too far away and you will have to shout to be heard, too close and you will crowd the other person and make them uncomfortable. Take your cues from your partner.
- **Weight shifting** - shifting your weight as you sit or stand.
- **Leg crossing** - crossing your legs towards someone indicates a liking for them and wish to include them.

- **Breathing rate and depth** - breathing shallowly and quickly when the other person breathes slowly and deeply will indicate a disconnect between the two of you. Mirror their breathing patterns to put you both on the same wavelength.
- **Voice tempo** - How quickly you speak. Quick speaking can be difficult to comprehend and relate to if someone is accustomed to speaking and listening slowly, and taken the other way around it can be frustrating.
- **Tone**
- **Inflection**
- **Cadence**
- **Volume** - how loud you are speaking.
- **Hesitation and pauses** - some people speak more hesitantly than others, with pauses between thoughts or phrases. Recognize and respect their speech patterns, and adapt. Talking over someone in conversation because they paused for a breath will not endear you to them.
- **Metaphors** - take your cues from the other person as far as using metaphors goes. If they seem to be very literal, don't use using too many metaphors when you talk.
- **Expressions and jargon** - in situations where some people have very specialized knowledge and some do not (for example, an event where half of the attendees are heart surgeons and the other half are not involved in medicine)

be careful about using expressions and jargon that your conversational partner may not be familiar with. It is off-putting for someone to have to ask you to explain a word or term too many times.

- **Word choice** - some people may be very formal in their speech, some may use more colloquial phrases or terms of speech. Note the words your conversation partner uses language, and model your language on his or hers.

As you can see, there are many aspects of your partner's behavior that you can mirror. You can mirror some or all of these items when building rapport, but be careful to keep mirroring from sliding into mimicking. Repeating what the other person does or says exactly is irritating and off-putting. If you have trouble distinguishing between the two, remember the game that small children play to annoy each other, when they repeat everything the other says and does. Do not be that small child.

Keep the mirroring general - for example, you can match their breathing pattern, but do not obviously take a deep breath each time they do. It can make the other person uncomfortable, and be counterproductive in your attempt to build rapport.

In a corollary to mirroring, it is useful to know how to consciously mismatch. This is the opposite of mirroring, when that you deliberately change your body language or speech patterns so that you and your conversational partner are no longer on the same wavelength. When done consciously and deliberately, mismatching is useful for signaling the end of a conversation or encounter, because the other participant will respond to your signals and recognize that your conversation is over. Once you have mismatched, don't walk away without saying goodbye. Leave an opening for follow-up contact to continue the acquaintance and strengthen your rapport.

- **Leading**

Leading is continues the concept of mirroring, but in a way that allows you to take control of the situation. Leading occurs when you and another mirror each other and you can get them to follow your lead in the mirroring process. This technique works best when you are already on your way to establishing a rapport, and wish to continue or test the strength of the rapport you have already built.

To practice the leading technique, select a behavior of the other person that you are mirroring, such as posture. Mirror that behavior for a while, and then begin to make incremental changes to your behavior (for example, if you were both slouching, begin to slowly straighten up).

Watch to see if, as you do this, the other person begins to change their posture to mirror yours. If they do, you have successfully established a rapport and established yourself as a leader in your interaction.

- Asking questions

Asking questions is one of the most important things you can do to build a rapport with someone. Remember, you don't want the conversation to be all about you, you want to focus the conversation on them.

The best way to focus the conversation on the other person and learn more about them is to ask them questions. However, these need to be the right kinds of questions. Questions which can be answered with a simple "Yes" or "No" do not help build rapport. The questions you ask should be open-ended, so that the other person can explain and expound on their topic. "How did you get into your field?" "What was your favorite part of that vacation?" and "What do you consider your greatest accomplishment?" are all open-ended and encourage the person being asked to go into detail on the topic.

Also, once the person has answered the question, ask a follow-up question based on their answer. The more questions you ask and they answer, the more likely it is that you will hit upon a common experience or area of interest that you can talk about with them.

While the idea of asking questions build a rapport is fairly common, Andrew Sobel in his book <u>Power Questions: Build Relationships, Win New Business, and Influence Others</u> developed the idea of asking questions as a basis of rapport building and came up with the concept of "power questions." Power questions are "provocative, specific, open-ended question that really allows a person to open up to you and feel as if you care about what they have to say." They continue our previous idea of asking open-ended, non-yes-or-no questions to keep the conversation going and learn more about the other person, while keeping attention in the conversation firmly on them. In Power Questions, Sobel developed a framework for developing rapport using power questions.

The framework looks like this:

1. Order an answer (ie: "So, tell me...")
2. Repeat it back.
3. Power question.
4. Use verbing to avoid getting stuck.
5. Bring in the feelings.

This framework uses many of the concepts that we have already discussed as strategies to develop rapport.

In a variation on the "ask question" strategy, Sobel recommends ordering questions, which you do by ordering information rather than asking a question. In this paradigm, the question "What was your favorite part of your weekend" would be rephrased as "So, tell me about your favorite part of your weekend." According to Sobel, this establishes your control over the conversation and shows that you're asking out of interest, not out of obligation.

The "repeat it back" step of Sobel's framework is the same as the "mirroring" concept we have already discussed. It consists of summarizing what the other person said and repeating is back to them, like in our earlier example of "so, you went to Peru and the mountain climbing was awesome." Again, this technique shows that you are paying attention and establishes understanding between you and the person you're conversing with.

After you repeat what the other person has said, ask a power question – a specific, open-ended question about what they just told you. This question should keep the conversation rolling, and give you more material for your next power question. People like to talk about themselves and what they know best, so once you've gotten on a fruitful topic, keep the questions coming. You'll learn a great deal about your partner, and they will feel appreciated.

If for some reason the conversation stalls, Sobel recommends "verbing." This is a quick technique for thinking up new question, and involves taking something that your partner has said and asking a question about it. For example, if they said they went for a walk, ask about their walk. This technique is designed to keep the momentum of the conversation going. Awkward, unfilled silences when you and your partner are both waiting for the other to say something can kill rapport quickly. Using this technique can help you avoid that particular disaster.

The final step of Sobel's rapport framework is to bring in feelings, and this can be tricky. To bring in the feelings, you can develop a conversation further by asking how something felt or saying how you would have felt in that situation. For example, if the other person tells you about climbing to the top of a really difficult mountain, you can say "wow, you must have felt really happy" or ask "how did that feel?" Sharing emotional responses with someone is an effective way to create or strengthen a bond. However, if an emotional comment or question is brought in too soon in the conversation or rapport-building, it can be perceived as awkward and nosy, and can turn the other person off. Bringing emotion into play can be risky, but correctly used it has great rewards. It is up to you to determine whether this particular technique is appropriate for a given situation.

- Establishing common ground

Establishing common ground is one of the best ways to build a rapport with someone. Discussing a shared interest or similar history allows you to bond over the common theme. The previously discussed technique of asking questions is a great way to find out if you and your conversational partner have anything in common. Using one technique can lead straight to another, and they build on each other to increase your ability establish a rapport. Once you find out you have something in common, stay on that topic. If you find you both have vacationed in the same place, ask what their favorite part of the trip was and tell an anecdote of your own. People are quicker to respond and build a rapport if they perceive you as like them, or part of their tribe. Establishing common ground activates this shortcut.

- **Practicing Quid Pro Quo**

Quid pro quo is a great technique for both building rapport in both the initial conversation and later interactions. In the initial conversation, while you want to focus your energy and your part of the conversation on the other person, it is best to not let it get too one-sided. A good way to prevent this from happening is practicing quid pro quo.

When the other person shares something about themselves, share something about yourself. This is particularly important if rapport has built quickly and your conversation has reached an emotional level. The more personal or important the information that the other person is sharing, the more essential it is that you offer them something about yourself in exchange.

In interactions after the initial conversation, quid pro quo can take several forms.

People are hardwired to reciprocate when others do them favors. If you do a favor for the person you are building rapport with, it is likely to be reciprocated. You can then reciprocate from that favor and being to build a relationship on the mutual favor-exchange. Keep in mind that these favors do not have to be material or large. Making an introduction, giving feedback or acting as a soundboard are just as legitimate for quid pro quo as assisting on a project or providing some kind of needed resource.

- Asking for Help

Asking for help is a rapport technique that builds on the same foundation as quid pro quo, but approaches it from the other way. Asking for help for a small matter builds a rapport between you and the person you ask, because doing a favor for someone makes you feel more positive about that person. Taking advantage of this knowledge by asking for help in a small matter helps create positive feelings toward you and builds your rapport.

Similarly to the quid pro quo technique, the item you ask for help with does not need to be physical or material. Asking for someone's advice or opinion is just as effective as asking for help on a project or asking for help to find something.

One word of warning for this particular technique - keep the item you ask for help with small and simple. Help that is easy for the other person to give is the best for developing positive feelings on the part of the helper, but the moment the other person feels as if you're placing them under a burden or obligation the positive feelings evaporate. If people feel as if you are taking advantage of them and the interaction, their participation in the rapport-building will end, and the participant will walk away with negative feelings towards you instead of positive ones.

This is particularly true if you are in a work environment and building a rapport with someone higher up in your company or business. Be careful not to give them impression that you are trying to get as much out of them as you can get. This is not the way to build a rapport that will develop into a long-term relationship.

Rapport-building Behaviors

We've established several techniques one can use to build rapport. Now, we can delve into more specific behaviors that assist in building rapport. These behaviors can be applied in any situation, whether you are engaging in conversation or in some more active activity. These behaviors are both physical and conversational, and include:

Physical Behaviors:

- **Keep your body language open and attentive.** Don't cross your arms or legs or tap your feet. Keep your body turned towards the person you are talking to and your head facing them, and if you are sitting, lean forward.

- **Look at the other person for approximately 60% of the time.** Give plenty of eye-contact but be careful not to make them feel uncomfortable. Prolonged staring or unbroken eye contact can make other people extremely uncomfortable and be seen as a challenge.

- **Smile.** This helps to keep the interaction consistently positive.

- **Keep good posture.** It reinforces positivity, energy, and enthusiasm.

- **Speak slowly.** You want the other person to be able to understand you, and you don't want to appear stressed.

- **Do not fidget.** Do not check or fiddle with your phone, or be constantly scanning the crowd or looking at others parts of the room. You want to give the other person your undivided attention.

Conversational Behaviors:

- **Use the other person's name at least once in the conversation.** This both reinforces how your attention is focused on them and helps you remember their name in the future.

- **Do not one-up the other person.** If they are telling a funny story, do not try to top it with a funnier one. Remember, you are trying to build a rapport, not score conversational points.

- **Greet people when you see them.** To build rapport in the long-term, greet people properly when you see them. Saying "hello" along with a smile confirms that you know and like the person you're greeting, even if you don't have time to stop for a full conversation. This builds positivity and connection between you and the other person.

- **Be honest if you don't know something.** Admit when you don't know the answer or have made a mistake. Being honest is always the best tactic, and acknowledging mistakes or ignorance will help to build trust, particularly when it is likely that you will called out by prior or superior knowledge.

- **Have an exit strategy from the conversation.** You do not want to linger awkwardly after your subjects of conversation have been exhausted or past the point where you have the interest of the other person. Base your exit strategy on the circumstances you're in, and also have several backup exit lines in case the initial one you pick is no longer applicable or appropriate after your conversation. Common exit strategies include having to get a drink, seeing someone you need to meet, having to leave the event you're at, and needing to run to the restroom. It is effective to combine this behavior with deliberate mismatching, to indicate both verbally and physically that your interaction is at an end.

- **When the interaction stops, leave the conversation open.** Pick something that the other person has told you and say that you would love to hear more about it. This keeps the line of communication open and reiterates your interest in the other party.

- **Be genuine.** This is important. People will be able to tell if you are faking enthusiasm or interest, depending on your acting ability, and few things turn people off as quickly. Be genuine in your interaction or your will lose the chance at the rapport you wanted.

Finally, keep your interaction appropriate to the conversation and circumstance. Even if you have been building a strong rapport with another person, if you introduce a behavior, language, or topic of conversation that is inappropriate for the circumstances, this budding rapport can be destroyed.

This is particularly true in work-related circumstances. Avoid conventionally risky topics, such as politics, religion, and money. While humor can be a great tool for building rapport, avoid jokes that could be considered off-color.

Chapter 4
The Relationships of Rapport

Once you have established a rapport, you can build on it to create a more established, lasting relationship. This is how rapport develops into friendship, love, and strong relationships with coworkers and clients that pay dividends financially and in quality of life and work in the long term. Rapport is the first step to establishing these kinds of bonds.

Below, we will take a look at how to take rapport the next step to relationships, and discuss the various kind of relationships that can develop and how to build into each.

Rapport to Friendship

Developing rapport into friendship is one of the most basic ways to develop a relationship from rapport. Most other relationships that you will develop have their basis, in some way, on friendship. Successful romantic relationships will have a an element of friendships, successful marriages will have a strong element of friendship, and the most effective coworker relationships will have an element of friendship as well.

To build on the positive, caring, and understanding connection that is rapport, it is best to create as many encounters with the other person as possible to continue the connection, and to build upon that initial rapport, follow up to suggest meeting for an activity that you will both enjoy. For the best result, this activity should be related to your previous conversation.

For example, if the person talked about how much he or she enjoys gardening, suggest an outing to a local botanical gardens (or similar locale, depending on the available options). It's best to position these encounters to take advantage of special events or deals, both to have a good reason to suggest that particular activity and to give the impression that you heard about the event, thought of the other person, and remembered their interest in that topic or activity. This will leave the other person with the gratifying impression that you were paying attention during the conversation, remembered their particular interest, and want to share it with them.

The more activities you and other person can do together and the more time you spend with each other, the more the rapport will build into a friendship, and the more solid the friendship will become.

During these follow-up encounters, continue to use the recommended rapport-building behaviors, particularly the physical behaviors. While the conversational behaviors may change according to the circumstances, continuing physical behaviors that give off attentiveness, openness, and positivity is a good move for any degree of rapport or friendship.

Rapport to Romantic Relationship

Developing a rapport into a romantic relationship is similar to developing one into a friendship, with several added components.

As with developing a friendship, to develop an initial rapport into a romance, you need to create as many encounters with the other person as possible. Suggesting a meeting or activity based on a previously expressed interest on the part of the other person pays even more dividends in a developing romantic relationship than it does in a developing friendship, since the caring and attentiveness aspects of a romantic relationship are even more important than they are for a developing friendship.

Continuing the relationship past friendship will involve physical and romantic attraction on the part of the other person that you cannot control. However, touching can be used to help develop a physical rapport into something deeper. Intermittent small touches - on the shoulder, on the hand, brushing the other when you stand next to them - helps to make someone feel comfortable near you, indicates affection and interest, and help to build excitement and anticipation around you. Build this small touching behavior slowly. Too much touch, too soon can cross boundaries and not be socially acceptable.

Building physical rapport through touch and continuing to practice mirror and reframe when your rapport has been established with help translate that rapport into a relationship, in the right circumstances.

Rapport to Work Relationship

A great working relationship with your coworkers, clients, bosses, and any people you manage is one of the most powerful indicators of a good work environment and a happy working life. Not only do work relationships make working more fun, these kinds of relationships also make it easier and more successful.

Work relationships can be friendships, but they can also be relationships of trust and mutual respect that have not developed into personal friendship. For example, you can have a great working relationship with a coworker, depend on their assistance, and trust them to take care of important project without wanting to invite them to your cookout or your child's birthday party.

To build this kind of relationship, consistency is key. You have established a rapport that indicates mutual understanding and interest, now you need to establish that past the personal rapport, you can be trusted with things that are important to the other person's professional life.

To develop trust in the workplace, it is best to take advantage of the rapport you have established to ask for or offer help with a small matter. Once you have done that, practice the quid pro quo technique. Reciprocate assistance with the other person as often as you can, and do your best to make sure whatever you assisted with goes well. Follow up with the other person to either ask how something turned out or to tell them the results of something they assisted with.

The person will appreciate your continued interested and being kept in the loop, and the follow-up conversation itself will lead to a closer rapport and relationship between you, particularly if you continue to practice the techniques described above.

Rapport to Successful Marriage

Rapport is definitely not the only secret to a successful marriage, and if you're married to someone, you have probably already established a rapport with them. However, people can grow apart or allow their rapport to lose steam and go stale.

In the case of marriage, it is good practice to continually build rapport all over again. Talking with your spouse, paying attention, listening, and finding common ground are all highly recommended by marriage counselors, and it's not a coincidence that they just happen to be the main techniques of building rapport.

When rebuilding rapport with your spouse, it's likely that you know a great deal about them already. However, it's not possible to know everything.

Pick a new development, and use the power questions technique to learn as much as you can about this development and, by extension, your spouse. Practice the quid pro quo technique if your discussion leads to sharing emotions or more personal information, exactly as if you were building rapport with someone new.

Relationships are like buildings, they need to be constantly fixed, rebuilt, and renewed, or they will weaken and crumble. Practicing rapport-building with your spouse on a consistent basis shores up the foundation and helps to repair any weak spots in the "walls."

Maintaining the Relationships

Maintaining a relationship is usually a matter of continuing to use the techniques and behaviors that established the rapport in the first place. Like developing rapport into a relationship, the best way to keep rapport is to create encounters with and spend time with the other person so that you have an opportunity to maintain and fuel the rapport.

While some people have a rapport that is strong enough to go months without seeing each other, and then naturally fall into easy communication and a deep rapport when they see each other again, this is not a common occurrence. If possible, try to see the person you are building a rapport with at regular intervals, and when you see them, continue your earlier conversations.

While you schedule your meetings or events with the person you initially developed a rapport with, don't forget that your behavior during the meetings is just as essential for maintaining and building on the rapport as having the meetings.

In other words, to maintain the rapport you've established, you need to do more than just show up. Over the course of your meetings, share increasing amounts of yourself with your rapport-partner. Practice quid pro quo, and have the give and take be about more personal subjects.

For example, recall the fifth step in the Power Questions technique. This step is called "bring on the feelings" and it encourages you to ask about and share feelings about an event or experience with the other person, because sharing feelings connects you with another person quickly and closely. However, in Power Questions Andrew Sobel warns to be careful using this step, as introducing emotion into a rapport too quickly can be a turn-off for some individuals. Since this is a powerful technique that one should not use too early in the rapport-building process, it is a perfect tool to use for maintaining rapport. Introducing emotion into a rapport, via questions or other avenues, is a great way to deepen the rapport and ensure that it continues to grow.

One of the best ways to fuel rapport is to remember interests, events, and hobbies that the other person mentioned, and ask about them or mention subjects relating to them when you see each other again. This shows that you paid attention and care, which creates a positive bond between the two of you.

Continuing a previous example, if someone you are building a rapport with mentions that they enjoy gardening or flowers, arrange your next get-together to be at a botanical gardens or some other locale that matches their interest. Not only will this demonstrate your attention and interest, it also sets a positive tone for the rest of the encounter.

While you both have positive feelings towards the other, reinforcing this positivity with a demonstration of your interest, and ensuring your encounter will take place in a location or at an event that will put the other person in a positive frame of mind, takes some of the responsibility for establishing initial positivity off of your behavior. In other words, it's a shortcut to making the other person happy with you.

For the rest of the follow-up encounters, make sure to keep practice the techniques and behaviors that you utilized during the initial meeting and to develop the initial rapport. Mirror the other person's physical and verbal behaviors and cues, maintain eye contact, pay attention while the other person is speaking, and do your best to establish more common ground with every encounter.

Chapter 5
The Applications of Rapport

While it is useful to know the background to, importance of, and techniques for building rapport, the benefits of rapport are not felt until you've actually used it.

There are three main areas of life that are best for building rapport: at work, at home, and in your social life. There are many different scenarios for developing and applying rapport in these areas, and situations will rarely be the same for different people. Even within similar work environments or home lives, each person's interactions are unique, and people approach situations differently.

Try to stay flexible, and pick and choose which techniques and skills sets are appropriate for situations as they arise.

At Work

Applying rapport at work ranges from helpful to essential for career success, depending on the field you work in and the position you hold. How rapport is applied and how important it is will be different for an independent plumber than for a teacher in a primary school or a hiring manager at an accounting firm.

What rapport does reliably do, in any field or position, is enhance working relationships so you'll enjoy increased success.

Below are some example of rapport that can develop at work among different people in different fields, and how rapport affects both the job and performance.

In business, the most common work environment is the traditional office setting. In this setting, rapports can develop between people in a number of different positions. Examples include rapport between coworkers at the same level, between managers and those they supervise, between a business person and a client, and between a hiring manager and someone being interviewed.

Coworker to coworker rapport fosters trust and a sense of community, and the people involved are more likely to help and support each other. This in turn results in a positive work environment and a more effective office overall, since the employees will pool their abilities and resources.

A rapport between a supervisor or boss and an employee or someone he or she supervises is just as important, but the effects are slightly different. If there is a rapport between a boss and employee, the relationship is likely to be more productive, because the employee will work harder for someone they have a rapport with than someone that they merely work for.

A rapport between a business person and a client is usually more formal than a rapport between coworkers and employees, but developing a rapport with a client means that there is a much greater chance of getting repeat business and more clients through recommendations than if someone does not cultivate the client and develop a rapport with them, which hopefully leads to a working relationship.

It is extremely important that hiring managers and interviewers in the business world be able to quickly develop rapport. According to a human resources management toolkit from the Wentworth Institute of Technology, rapport is "essential to the interview process as [it allows] the job applicant to feel comfortable from the start of the interview while serving the larger purpose of determining whether or not the job candidate will be a great fit." (Source: http://www.wit.edu/human-resources/manager-corner/toolkit/Rapport-Building.pdf.)

Rapport between an interviewer and interviewee is developed according to most of the same techniques as other professionals use in the workplace, with an additional emphasis on the importance of appearance and first impressions for the interviewee. Interviewees may only get one chance to develop a rapport with the interviewer, so first impressions are more important for them than they are for other professionals who can develop their rapport over multiple interactions. While dress and appearance are important for developing rapport in an interview, techniques such as mirroring and establishing common ground, as well as the other specific rapport-building behaviors we have described, are essential for building a rapport part the initial, five-second first impression.

While it is useful and occasionally essential to be able to build rapport in business, there are fields where the development of rapport is significantly more central to succeeding. In the field of medicine, the ability of doctors and nurses to develop a rapport with their patients can determine whether or not they will learn everything they need to know about the patient's condition and symptoms. A patient who feels a connection to their doctor is more likely to tell them everything, and correspondingly more likely to follow directions set by a doctor.

Rapport between doctors, between nurses, and between doctors and nurses also directly impacts the patient's medical care, since a medical team that works well together will be far more effective and cooperative than one made up of people who do not feel any kind of connection with their coworkers.

In medicine, establishing common ground is probably the best and fastest way for doctors assigned to the same case or on the same team to establish a rapport.

Mirroring behavior and verbal cues are also great techniques to employ, particularly if you are pressed for time. Asking for help is the third technique to consider employing to develop rapport quickly in a high-pressure environment, if the help you ask for is small and not burdensome or time-consuming.

Remember, in medicine, your colleagues are busy. Asking for assistance on something that proves to be time-consuming or burdensome will not build rapport. Instead, it will most likely leave them with feelings of resentment, and annoyance that you did not respect their time.

A second field in which success can depend on your ability to develop rapport is teaching. The ability of a teacher to connect with his or her students and build the kind of relationship of caring and trust that rapport entails can determine how successful his or her students are and how well-received his or her class or subject matter is. Students who feel like their teachers genuinely care about them and are interested in them usually do better in class, and are more willing to try harder and go the extra mile than they are for a teacher who they do not feel an emotional connection to.

An article in the Association for Psychological Science *Observer* by William Buskist and Bryan Saville of Auburn University entitled "Rapport-Building: Creating Positive Emotional Contexts for Enhancing Teaching and Learning" suggests that the kind of rapport that great teachers and their students enjoy is not the result of doing any one thing, but instead is "the result of many things done consistently right." They go on to suggest several things teachers can do to try to build a rapport with their students, cautioning that picking just one will not be enough, and that teachers need to consistently use a combination of these suggestions in order to build a rapport.

The suggestions are:

- Learn to call your students by name.
- Learn something about your students' interests, hobbies, and aspirations.
- Create and use personally relevant class examples.
- Arrive to class early and stay late - and chat with your students.
- Explain your course policies - and why they are what they are.
- Post and keep office hours.
- Get on line - use e-mail to increase accessibility to your students.
- Interact more, lecture less - emphasize active learning.
- Reward student comments and questions with verbal praise.
- Be enthusiastic about teaching and passionate about your subject matter.
- Lighten up - crack a joke now and then.
- Be humble and, when appropriate, self-deprecating.
- Make eye contact with each student - without staring, glaring, or flaring.
- Be respectful.
- When all else fails, smile a lot - students will think you like them and your job.

(Buskist and Saville, March 2001).

There are many other roles and positions in many, many fields which either require rapport-building skills for success or are helped by the ability to develop a rapport with the people around them.

Human resources, hospitality, negotiations, and sales are all fields that require rapport-building skills. Whether someone is coaching a new hire, managing a five-star hotel, mediating two sides of an argument, or trying to talk a customer into buying a new car, establishing rapport makes their job significantly easier.

At Home

Applying rapport at home does not usually affect things like financial success or business performance, but it can make a huge difference in quality of life. At home, people are likely to build rapports with their spouses or significant others and potentially with their children (if they have any). Building rapport helps create a healthy and caring home life and deepens and strengthens relationships.

We have discussed the steps to and benefits of creating a continual spouse to spouse rapport, and how it helps maintain healthy marriage and relationships. Establishing rapport with your children has a similar number of benefits.

To begin with, within many families, the relationship between parent and child is the one close relationship in which neither party chose the other. If your child is your biological child, their tiny personhood is presented as something of a fait accompli, and both parties have to work with what they have.

Note, this is not the case for families in which the children are adopted - in this case, the parents and children can actually choose each other, which means that these families start at a different point when developing rapport between the parents and children.

Building a rapport with your child or children as early and as consistently as possible helps to develop a strong relationship with them from an early age, and being consistent about rapport-building throughout your child's childhood keeps that relationship strong. This kind of strong, healthy parent-child relationship leads to more effective parenting, particularly when the child gets into the usually more difficult preteen and teenage years. Establishing a caring, understand bond is will make them more likely to listen to you and follow your instructions and advice.

In building and maintaining a rapport with a child, the techniques you use may vary as the child ages or depending on circumstances. Certain aspects of mirroring, particularly breath matching, are useful in the earliest years. However, rapport-building really starts when the child is old enough to be capable of having a conversation. When this occurs, the verbal mirroring, or reframing technique will be one of the most long-term effective techniques to create and maintain parent-child rapport.

Verbal mirroring – or reframing – will allow the parent to repeat back what they understood the child to say, so that the child can confirm whether or not the parent understood correctly and knows that the parent was listening to and understands what the child said.

Asking questions, particularly power questions, is another effective technique for building parent-child rapport, though as the child gets older they may start to see these question as intrusive. If that happens, and the question is not immediately important or essential, it is best to fall back on active listening and reframing as the most consistent parent-child rapport techniques.

In Social Life

Rapport is the basis of the connections that make up a social life. Friendship stems from initial rapport and is developed by building on existing rapport. Dating is based on physical attraction and initial rapport, and to develop into sometime more long-term, it is the rapport that really needs to develop.

The ability to build rapport is most obvious when meeting new people, in large groups, and in the dating scene. Some people can walk up to someone and develop a connection right away, and these people usually have a lot of good friends and are successful in the dating scene. As we've seen, this kind of immediate success can learned, through developing your rapport-building skills.

When you're developing new friendships, mirroring, asking questions, and establishing common ground are the most effective at developing rapport in one go if you are at a bar or a party.

To develop the rapport into a friendship, you should schedule or arrange follow-up events so you can continue to build the rapport. Asking for help, while an effective tool in the workplace, may not be as effective while developing new friendships, since using this technique may give the impression that you are attempting to take advantage of the rapport you've established.

When dating, you may use different rapport-building techniques based on the outcome you are hoping for.

Mirroring is an effective technique for any outcome, and physical mirroring can be a natural lead into developing a physical rapport, which is based on touch rather than words. Physical rapport was described in the earlier section on developing rapport into romance, and is developed through an intermittent string of small touches. Repeated touches on the hand or arm show interest, and this form of touching is a way to make a potential partner comfortable with you and generate excitement.

If you are in a situation that allows for conversation, asking questions is an excellent technique to use because it lets you focus your attention on your date, learn about him or her, and find ways to establish common ground.

Now it may be difficult to use the technique of asking questions if you are in an area with a great deal of loud music or other noise, like a party, crowded bar, or concert. In this situation, it is best to develop the physical rapport through mirroring, touching, and facial expression, and allow verbal rapport to wait to be developed until you are in more conducive, quieter circumstances.

Chapter 6
The Practices of Rapport

While you've learned how to build rapport, learning something conceptually and putting it into practice can be two very different things. Of course, the best way to become good at something is to practice, and rapport-building is no exception. You can go out and practice the techniques we've discussed in the field, but it is easier to practice new skills in a controlled environment.

There are some rapport-building activities and exercises that you can use to both practice building rapport on your own, and implement when you need a group or team to build rapport quickly.

Rapport-building Activities and Exercises

Ice-breakers and team-building activities are not the time-wasters that many think. They are actually designed to help people build rapport quickly, and are therefore often used when a group of people is working together closely to accomplish a common goal. Rapport between team members fosters cooperation, creativity, and an atmosphere of mutual regard and assistance, which help teams accomplish their goals more quickly, more thoroughly, and more successfully.

Some rapport-building activities that include:

- **Group Identity (Group exercise).**

Create a common identity for a team or group by asking them to decide on an entertaining name that is based on something they all have in common. For example, if they are all parents and all love winter sports, their name might be "Ice Ice Baby."

- **Pacing Mismatch (Group exercise).**

Putting people in groups of four, and ask them to take time to observe and write down whether the other group members are fast talkers or slow talkers. Then pair a fast talker and a slow talker together, and have them hold an imaginary business meeting. Next, pair a fast talker and fast talker together (or a slow talker and slow talker) and have them hold the exact same imaginary business meeting. Ask the participants whether they noticed the difference in difficulty communicating and rapport between when they were paired with someone who moved at their own pace and someone with a mismatched pace. This exercise helps to highlight the importance of mirroring during rapport-building.

- Practice Mirroring (Partner exercise).

You and a partner can sit down and practice the mirroring technique. Take note of your partner's posture, breathing, and vocal cues, and match your behavior to theirs. It will probably feel awkward at first, but the practice will pay dividends when you find yourself establishing rapport with an increasing number of people more and more quickly. If it helps, give each other feedback, particularly if anything your partner is doing makes you uncomfortable, and vice versa. The feedback will be particularly helpful if you have a tendency to mimic instead of mirror. Your partner will catch you, and you will be able to correct your technique.

- Mirroring and Questioning (Individual exercise).

As an exercise you can do by yourself, find a picture of someone (it can be a hard copy or on the internet). Note how that person is standing or sitting and mirror their position. Then take five minutes to write down a list of possible things you could say to that person to being a conversation and build rapport. Use visual cues from the location, dress, company, and objects around the person in the picture to come up with questions, and make sure to keep them rapport-building (i.e. open-ended power questions). Once your five minutes it up and you have your initial questions, select your favorite and write down two follow-up questions that you can use, depending on their hypothetical response. This exercise will help you observe physical cues about someone, practice develop rapport-building questions, and practice physical mirroring.

- **Communication Examination (Partner exercise).**

Step 1:
Sit down with another person and spend five minutes talking about any subject. Once the five minutes it up, each answer the following questions:

1. How do I usually communicate?
2. How do I usually speak?
3. How do I usually express myself?
4. How do I best understand something when it is presented to me?

Then, pick up another piece of paper and study your neighbor.

1. How does he/she usually communicate?
2. How does he/she speak?
3. How does he/she express himself/herself
4. How does she best understand something when it is presented to him/her?

Step 2:
Review the answers to each set of questions together. If you answered any differently, discuss why.

This exercise will give you great insights into your mode of communication and expression, and help you practice being sensitive to the communication styles and preferences of others. The more you know about yourself and the more easily you can identify how another person operates, the easier it will be to adapt your style to theirs and build rapport.

- **Finding Similarities (Group exercise).**

Have a group of six or so people sit in a circle, and take five minutes to determine ten ways that they are all similar to each other. These similarities can be anything, from everyone liking ice cream to everyone speaking Spanish. The similarity itself is not important, what is important is that you are establishing common ground, one of the best and quickest ways to build rapport.

****

This list is not exhaustive. There are many exercises, activities, and ice-breakers out there that either help to build rapport, help practice building rapport, or help practice one aspect or technique of rapport-building. Using these exercises to practice connecting and communicating with others will quickly build your communication skills, and you will notice how quickly you establish new, valuable connections or rekindle old rapports.

Chapter 7
The Establishment of Rapport

Rapport, and the ability to develop it with another person, is essential for developing the long- and short-term relationships that lead to a great quality of life and increase the odds of business and financial success.

While some people have a natural gift for building rapport with others, this is a talent that can be learned, and anyone can develop the skill set needed to quickly and meaningfully connect with another person.

Using techniques such as mirroring, reframing, asking questions, asking for help, establishing common ground, and quid pro quo, rapport-building can become a key asset in social and work-related development.

Studies conducted by scientists, researchers, and psychologists have established the usefulness and importance of rapport in medicine, law, negotiation, politics, international relations, and teaching. Great teachers, successful businessmen and salespeople, and effective psychologists and other medical practitioners at least partly owe their successes to their abilities to establish rapport with their students, patients, and clients.

Rapport has become such a recognized component of success that publications like Forbes.com and Entrepreneur.com have taken to examining the different ways to establish and benefit from rapport with clients and customers. Articles on the subject include "New Ways Business Leaders Are Building Rapport With Clients Outside of the Office" by Rachel Weingarten and "Strategies for Establishing Rapport with the Affluent" by Russ Alan Prince on Forbes.com, and "3 Ways to Use Social Media to Build Rapport With Your Customers" by Bridget Gleason and "Here's How to Strike Up A Conversation with Almost Anyone" by Jacqueline Whitmore.

These are only a few examples of the multiplicity of popular publications and resources that have established rapport firmly in the common lexicon of success, and try to make its advantages available to everyone.

Scholarly articles, books, how-tos, and popular articles like the ones mentioned above barely scratch the surface of the wealth of information on building and benefitting from rapport in almost any situation.

Once someone understands how important and teachable rapport is, he or she can learn the techniques described above and practice them, both with the exercises and activities shown and on the ground, in networking and business events, parties, and with friends and in the home.

Finally, once the technique of building and maintaining rapport has been mastered, it is possible for everyone to get a piece of the success that rapport is enjoying and has bestowed on so many.

Rapport | Gabriel Angelo

About The Author

Gabriel Angel is the founder of SN & NS Publications, the publisher of multiple works within the realm of social dynamics, dating advice, and personal relationships. He is also an author, social scientist coach and expert focusing on breaking down the intricacies of interpersonal interactions and human behaviors with others. Be sure to look for his other works:

- Social Skills
The Modern Skill for Success, Fun, and Happiness Out of Life

- How to Overcome Social Anxiety
Proven Strategies to Get Rid of Social Anxiety and Take Control of Your Social Life

Made in the USA
Middletown, DE
12 January 2017